HENRY ANDREW JACKSON

Copyright © 2024 Henry Andrew Jackson

All rights reserved. No part of this publication may be reproduced, distributed, or transmitted in any form or by any means, including photocopying, recording, or other electronic or mechanical methods, without the prior written permission of the publisher, except in the case of brief quotations embodied in critical reviews and certain other noncommercial uses permitted by copyright law. For permission requests, write to the publisher, addressed "Attention: Permissions Coordinator," at the address below.

Paperback ISBN: 978-1-63616-228-7
eBook ISBN: 978-1-63616-230-0

Published By Opportune Independent Publishing Co.
www.opportunepublishing.com

Printed in the United States of America

For permission requests,
please email the publisher with the subject line as
"Attention: Permissions Coordinator" to the email address below:
Info@Opportunepublishing.com

CONTENTS

I Hope You Enjoy This Book	8
In Our Journey	9
How I Stand	10
For Me And You	11
Declare What Is Best	13
As I Serve The Lord	14
Be Reconciled	16
Receiving God's Grace	17
Be My Shield In All My Days	18
We Must Believe	19
This Poem Is About God	21
Yes, We Do Stand Tall	22
Cemetery Meeting, 2014	23
Homecoming Day At Piney	24
Plan, Work And Play	25
Touched By You, Holy Ghost	26
On The Cross	27
Easter Poem 2012	29
Coming Back	30
Rough Water Is Here	31
Your Pain Meant Our Glory	32
Reason For The Season	33
Witness For Christ	34
Praising Him; That's In Line	35
To Follow While He Leads	36

Caught In The Air	37
Our Help On High	38
To Overcome	39
Controlled By Love	40
My Talent I Must Use	41
Scripture About The Church	42
Steadfastness In Him	43
Prove Me Now	44
Captured But Now Free	45
As I Learn, Then I Move	46
We Can Make It	47
He Lives	48
Celebrating Jesus On Christmas Day	49
On Bended Knees	50
Favorite Scripture	52
Should Be Every Day	53
Why Me?	54
Praise To The Father On High	55
Neither Be Thou Dismayed	56
The Physician No One Seen	57
The One Way	58
Denied Although A Spotless Lamb	59
I Conquered It All For You	60
If I Shut Up Heaven	61

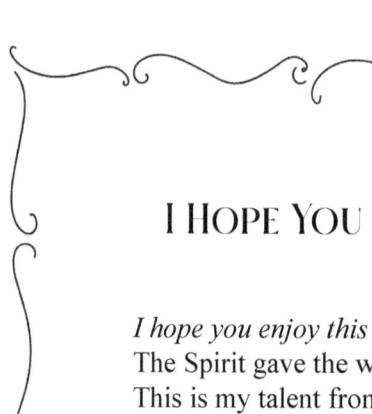

I Hope You Enjoy This Book

I hope you enjoy this book
The Spirit gave the words to me
This is my talent from God,
For I went from lost to free

If you are in need of something,
Take a minute and look around
Let the words enter your mind
So you can find solid ground

For with my pen in hand,
The Spirit soothes my soul
I set my thoughts on God,
My priority and my goal

God blessed me with this book
I'm highly favored today
His blessings are everlasting
He guides and directs my way

As I think about the Savior
I close my eyes in prayer
I felt like this is something
That I needed to share

So I proceed to follow God
Directing me to take a look
Since He gave me these words:

I hope you enjoy this book

Written 7-14-24, 6 a.m.

In Our Journey

We must get closer to God
Through prayer is how it will be done
Guidance from the Spirit and scripture
For in our journey, we've almost won

For as we follow, we press on
We look at the scriptures for strength,
Desiring His word for comfort
Knowing what is the breadth and length

For this journey we are on
It's getting brighter and brighter we see
For He pulled us out of darkness
How thankful we all should be

Let's dwell on scripture awhile
What instruction does it give to all
2 Peter 1:10 tells us to give diligence,
Ensuring us that we shall never fall

For as the scripture comes to life,
We can't be at ease today
We must declare in "Jesus saves"
Have you thought about His way

We must get closer to God
It's not difficult to comprehend
For we are still "In our journey"
We meet Jesus in the end

Written 4-29-24, 8:30 a.m.

HOW I STAND

As I write this poem,
Scripture will be firsthand,
For my dedication is true
This is how I stand,

For my spirit needs guidance
As I collect my thoughts inside,
I can do nothing without You
In Your presence, let me hide

For as I open up my bible,
It's You I seek, my Lord
I stretch my hands out, Jesus
That wisdom can be stored,

For precious is Your word
Let it be rooted and grounded in me,
For You brought me out of darkness
I praise You, for now, I am free

I serve You with gladness
It's the happiness that You give
I don't have that spirit of fear
I have that spirit to live

So, as this poem is finished,
I'm thankful to be in Your plan,
For this is what keeps me going
This is how I stand

Written 4-29-24 7:30 a.m.

For Me and You

As we read, we ponder
As all brightness comes into view,
Together, we see God's hand,
What He did for me and you

For we wandered around in sin,
Then conviction came our way
The Spirit told us we needed Jesus,
As then we were convinced to pray

We repeatedly ask the Lord
Salvation, Lord, that's what I need
Set up Your kingdom, dear Jesus
Plant in me Your seed

Then, as the prayer continued,
That peace and calmness came in
Reality surfaced, then I knew:
I just got born again

Joy, unspeakable and full of glory
That's what the scripture reveals
For the King of Kings had visited
I purchased Him who heals

I have reached that plateau
Where every human needs to reach
Come out of sin and be righteous,
That's what the bible does teach

You're not no sinner, as some say
Let that sink in through and through
Have you given thought to the scripture,
What He did "for me and you?

Declare What Is Best

Trials and troubles surround us
We have all kinds of tests
But Jesus tells us all,
Declare what is best

In our minds, we seek wisdom
As entanglement tries to overpower
We then pray, *Jesus, send the rain*
Give us that Holy Ghost shower

Can you hear the mighty rushing wind?
Does it make you fall to your knees?
Send down that comforter, dear Father
Captivate us in that breeze

Let Your greatness take over
Stabilizing our walk inside You
We are that nation Peter talked about
When he said *the chosen few*

We are to mount our wings as eagles,
Grasping what the word does say,
Considering who holds tomorrow,
Reserving the time, no delay

Do you feel like shouting, my friend?
Does His spirit want you to confess?
Do you know He owns your soul?
Today, declare what is best

Written 7-14-2024 @ 6:20 a.m.

AS I SERVE THE LORD

A certain calmness is upon me,
Bringing me into one accord
I just relax all my thoughts
As I serve the Lord

For that is what I cherish
With gratitude, I am blessed
For in the heart, I believed,
And with my mouth, I did confess

That Jesus Christ is Lord
He has redeemed my soul
I stopped being the boss
I gave Him total control,

For you and I were on that ship,
The waves and water being tossed
Then, Jesus came, saying, *Peace, be still*
Water subsided, saving us from being lost

Put us all in recovery
Our focus became clear,
Jesus standing with us, hand in hand
What have we to fear?

We see Jesus in His word
As His disciples gathered 'round
Jesus teaching about His death,
That He delivers to all who need to be found

Do you have victory over death?
Is His kingdom inside you stored?
Isn't it a delight to say,
As I serve the Lord?

Written 7-14-24 @ 5:15 a.m.

BE RECONCILED

As Jesus gave us all teachings,
Together, we had them compiled
He taught us all we need Him
We all must be reconciled

Lost and undone due to Adam
As he disobeyed God from start
From being perfect to then lost
They had a filthy and dirty heart

Then from Adam to Moses and Moses to Jesus,
Change was on the move
The sacrifice came down to save
He came to heal and reprove

The cycle of life had reappeared
We now had a new life we could join,
For repentance now was accepted
A brighter future now is going

There's a mansion now awaiting
That's being built by our King
King Jesus, He's the carpenter
For He does most anything

He saves, corrects and heals
Removes mischief and all things wild
He delivers to all salvation
As He says, *Be reconciled*

Written 7-12-24, 6am

Receiving God's Grace

We have characters in scripture
Decided they needed to make haste
They inclined their ears to understanding
On how to receive God's grace

It's through faith, Paul said
Ephesians 2 and 8, it does quote
Much knowledge Paul put out
He established it in every note

Grace is unmerited favor from God
He announces it in His word,
For we must think of things that are pure,
Not of things that are absurd

Carry us further, dear Jesus
Give us a glimpse of what's ahead
Secure our minds with knowledge
Give us extra knowledge to be led

For we all are His sheep
The leader takes us by the hand
Can you feel where the nails were placed?
Do you feel those tears expand?

He gave His life for you and me,
Knowing ahead what we would face
That's why accepting Him is priority
And receiving God's grace

Written 7-12-24 @ 6:45 a.m.

BE MY SHIELD IN ALL MY DAYS

First, always, *Good morning, Jesus*
I open my hands in praise
Keep Your guidance with me, Lord
Be my shield in all my days

In my years, You stand out
About Your love, I will share
When I didn't deserve compassion,
I still received Your care

On my knees, I find help
As meditate upon You,
For life is at its best
Knowing Your spirit guides me through

Deliverance is Your specialty
Salvation is a gift that's free
Repentance is the route to take
Out of darkness now you can flee

We claim victory through His name,
Declaring scripture in fine detail
We give honor and glory to our King,
For in Him, we will never fail

So, to you, brothers and sisters
Isn't it time to give Him praise?
Asking Him, *Guide us, dear Lord*
Be my shield in all my days

Written 2-9-24 @ 6:30 a.m.

We Must Believe

As we journey through life,
From darkness we've been relieved
We've been governed and directed by Jesus
Saying to all, *We must believe*

We have met the Savior
We're pressing forward in His name
Salvation has touched us all
No more being lost and ashamed

Jesus is a rewarder
For those seeking His face
Redemption, it draweth nigh
As we receive amazing grace

Praise to the Father on high
Looking down on His people today
He strengthens and carries us all,
Protecting and comforting in every way

For as He changed our direction,
Giving knowledge and enabling us to stand,
He's gone to prepare a place for us,
A plane trip leaving this land

Makes you want to jump and shout
Can't you feel the Holy Ghost around?
He supplies and fills every need
As His guidance surrounds

Do you love your Savior this morning?
Hey, pastor, don't you feel relieved?
As you told us all this last Sunday,
Congregation, we must believe

Written 2-27-24, 5:30 a.m.

This Poem Is About God

This poem is about God
All the achievements that He made
For the directions He declared
With foundations that He laid

For God is a spirit
For that's how we worship Him today
It is full speed ahead
In His guidance; no delay

As we all submit to Him
With hearts open and hands lifted high,
He tells us to honor and praise Him,
For it's to Him we all draw nigh

Can you take a few minutes for Him?
It's the greatest thing you'll ever do
Look at what He accomplished
He gave up His son for you

Praise Him this morning,
Thanking Him for another day,
Collecting your thoughts in reverence,
Pondering every word you say

As I finish with this last quotation,
Let's take His word and explore,
For this poem was about God,
The one we need more and more

Written 6-13-23, 6:30am

YES, WE DO STAND TALL

What a wonderful day
God has given us all
Celebrating the Jackson family reunion
And yes, we do stand tall

We stand tall toward our Maker,
For in God, we're made complete
For Acts says, *In Him, we live*
He makes life so sweet

As we follow Him in scripture,
He makes us all become new
Being the sacrifice of His Father,
He gave His life for me and you

Our love should be unending
Are you following Him real close?
In priority, He should be number one
Jesus, we love You the most

As we celebrate at our reunion,
Showing forth love to all,
From this Jackson to everyone,
Yes, we do stand tall

Written 8-31-19

CEMETERY MEETING, 2014

Can I Get an Amen?
How blessed are you and I?
Let me explain why, my friend
We all have the favor of God
Can I hear an amen?

As we gather at this meeting,
Can we be serious one minute?
If death happened to you today,
Your eternity, where would you spend it?

Jesus came to save us all
He holds the name above all names
Have you been cleansed by the King?
To salvation, have you laid claim?

Without holiness, I'm not going to make it.
That's why I call so frequent
Give me knowledge, dear Savior
Don't let me stay delinquent

My desire is to know You more
Centered in Your word, made new
Not satisfied with being the same
Desiring to be just like You

Help me, Lord, to be kind,
Walking straight until my end
When I leave this life into Yours,
Can I get an amen?

God bless you! Be blessed

Homecoming Day at Piney

Welcome to the homecoming!
As we worship on this day,
We are here praising our Savior
As we continue to follow His way

His guidance is what we seek
More of God is our concern
Desiring His spirit to captivate
Getting deeper inside His word

For there is none greater
None greater inside this land
As I walk, shadow me, Jesus
Don't let me fall; help me stand

As we praise You on this occasion,
Fulfill Your word in US
Correct us; give us understanding
In Your ways, raise our trust

Whatsoever things are honest
Let Your greatness sustain all
Remove all obstacles that can hinder
Taking away darkness, making it fall

It's Homecoming Day at Piney
We praise and worship You this day
That is our one and only desire
As we continue to follow Your way

Written 11-1-2015

PLAN, WORK AND PLAY

If we are to move ahead,
Let me explain the only way:
We must be totally determined
To plan, work and pray

We have been informed to do this
If we are to proceed
Just as the scripture tells us
In acts that we should take heed

Using the right approach,
Looking past flesh to the soul,
To study each question entirely
And staying in complete control

Forming a plan in the mind
Praying that the Spirit will convict
Let's revive in us that commitment
That help is needed to those that are sick

People really need the Lord
To let his word come first
That the water of life is here
That it will cure all that thirst

We have God on our side,
If trouble tries to block the way,
Let's all be obedient to his directions
That we all plan, work and pray

TOUCHED BY YOU, HOLY GHOST

To stir up my pure mind,
That is what I need most
I have this desire inside,
Touched by you, Holy Ghost

I need to be in your presence,
Accompanied by a heavenly host
Send this power from on high
Touched by you, Holy Ghost

Fulfill this need I have
Amount needed: a heavy dose
Teach me and guide me, my lord
Touched by you, Holy Ghost

I have obtained your salvation
That enables me to boast
I have been changed by you, Jesus
Touched by you, Holy Ghost

We need a worldwide revival,
Surrounding areas coast-to-coast
Conviction from your throne
Touched by you, Holy Ghost

This is a rush order petition,
For our departure is so close
Open us up; let us be filled
Touched by you, Holy Ghost

ON THE CROSS

The time was a time of sorrow
As a life was brutally tossed
But praise to God almighty
He is not still there on the cross

Friend, He is risen
The stone has been rolled away
No earthly situation could hold Him
He did not come here to stay

Do you know why He came?
Do you wonder where to put your trust?
Friend, He was slaughtered as a lamb
And for who? For all of us

As they beat Him up that hill,
For me, He took all that shame
But through his shame, I am born again
I will gladly walk in His name

Do you know the king of kings?
His life, what a capturing story
He died so that you and I could live
Came to earth, but his home was in glory

All I can say is thank you, Jesus
No words could tell you how I feel
Guide me and direct me, my Lord
Keep me inside your perfect will

Thank you for giving me this chance
That I can live and not be lost
For brothers and sisters, on this day,
He is not still there on the cross

Easter poem 2005

Easter Poem 2012

As we accept the word we have,
We thank you, Father and Son,
As we receive knowledge of John 3:16
How wonderful is Matthew 27:51

Let me explain to you why,
Just what happened that very day:
The sacrifice of the lamb was complete
The veil of the temple was moved away

She was rent from top to bottom
We now have a sacrificial lamb
The only begotten of the Father,
He is our great I a

Let's journey through the scripture
To understand it as Isaiah proclaimed
He was wounded for our transgression
Together, we all bow to His name

Do you love Him as you should?
Do you fall daily on your knees?
Do you know your life belongs to Him?
He bought it, being nailed to that tree

Why don't you thank Him for it right now
For all the work that He's done?
He will bless you till no end
Read it—Matthew 27:51

COMING BACK

As we all come together,
Let's focus on this one fact:
The one we are praising and singing about
Is soon to be coming back

As we sing glory, hallelujah,
His spirit encamps this place
Let's yield ourselves to Him
Give to Him open space

Allow the Holy One inside
Let Him bless and keep you close
Be submissive to his directions,
To His anointing and the Holy Ghost

Answer me one thing, if you will:
Are you ready for His return?
Today is the day of salvation
He is working on you to turn

For tomorrows are not promised
Clouds of darkness so dim
He is stretching forth His hand to you
Will you stretch yours to Him?

You see, He is the deliverer
He has whatever it is you lack
His mercy now is extended to all
But He is soon to be coming back

ROUGH WATER IS HERE

We love you, Lord and Savior,
More than words could ever apply
We are calling on you tonight, Lord,
In a request to you on high

In your word, you said, ask,
And in your word, we believe
We know we must rely on you
In order for us to achieve

Being your servants, Lord,
Father, we seek direction from you
We have run into this wall
We are being faced with what to do

Trials, troubles and tribulations
With a load of despair and dismay
We need the leadership you possess,
Guidance in your perfect way

The last days are upon us
We must draw closer to you,
For soon, you will be coming
To take out your chosen few

We submit to you totally,
For it is your hand that saves
For you see rough water is here
It is you that controls the waves

Your Pain Meant Our Glory

Thank You for wonderful counsel,
For creating such a story,
For we know on this day,
Your pain meant our glory

What You did for us
As the reality of it comes through,
It leaves you all to wonder,
How could anyone not love You?

I worship You, King of Kings
Until there is no end
I will carry my cross You took
With my departure from sin

My freedom did come
When I knelt to make that call
He is risen from the dead
High and lifted up for all

Is He your Lord and Savior?
Or are you saying, *Some other time*?
Denying what the Master is singing
Won't you come and dine?

I'm seated now by my Father
When I leave it, end of story
For yes, death was my pain
But for you, it meant glory

Written Easter 2013

Reason for the Season

If I may have your attention,
There is this story I'd like to tell
What is the reason for the season?
Is it prizes or Emmanuel?

Is it to get to go to Walmart,
Picking out that *just right* thing?
Or is it about a baby in a manger,
The oncoming king of kings?

Is it to get all those gifts,
Wondering where on earth they'll be stored?
Or do you think of a lady named Mary,
About to deliver our precious Lord?

I guess the season is about giving
It's about showing forth love, handling strife,
For you see, this baby born this day
Later would lay down His life

He died for you and I
That our eternal life could be won
Do you have that promise, my friend,
In knowing God's only begotten son?

He's the reason for the season
He's the truth, the light, the way
Without Him, this season wouldn't be possible
Merry Christmas to you all this day

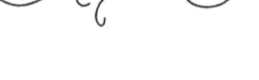

WITNESS FOR CHRIST

We exalt Your name, Jesus
Contact all through advice
Help us declare You Savior,
Being a witness for Christ

Lead me in Your paths
By the still waters upright
Teach me meekness and honor
That I can gain new sight

As we figure out our steps
To declare Him and make us new,
As we accept correction,
That correction washes us through

For we were all in bondage
Until God sent forth His son
To redeem this world through grace
In danger, we have none

For this reason, He saved us,
Giving all gifts from above
He gave His life for all
So He could fill us with His love

Let us get in His word,
For we were bought at a price
So, I will be telling all about Jesus,
Being a witness for Christ

Written 7-31-2024 @ 8 p.m.

Praising Him; That's in Line

Glory, Hallelujah to the Messiah
Thereis scripture we will find
As we read about our Savior
Praising Him; that's in line

That should be priority one:
Giving Him all praise
No matter the circumstances around,
A spiritual guide leads our days

We bow before our Savior
As He gives new hope within
We pray for mercy and guidance,
Not to let discouragement creep in

Shutting our eyes, do you picture Him
Sitting by His Father up above?
As we wonder about His return,
Do we feel His unwavering love?

For yes, He came to His own
They rejected Him, sending Him to a cross
Salvation now given to Gentiles
That we can now not die lost

We love You today, dear Jesus
In our journey, what we did find?
Don't you know he'd appreciate it?
Praising Him; that's in line

Written 7-25-24 @ 6:50 a.m.

TO FOLLOW WHILE HE LEADS

The Spirit accompanies life,
For in Jesus, we proceed
We are sheep, and in this, we know
To follow while He leads

We know who to follow
Jesus guides us; we can't cease,
For we are following the best,
Following the Prince of Peace

We took up our cross, praying through
As we entered into new life
He removed all sin abroad,
Taking away all anguish and strife

For what a Savior we serve
All the directions He does lay
He does all spiritual effects
All we must do is obey

When talking about directions,
Making sure the bible is our guide,
Study to shew thyself approved
Saying, *Jesus, in Your word, let me hide*

We know we have to call,
That we all can succeed
We all are sheep; we need help
To follow while He leads

Written 7-25-24 @ 7 a.m.

CAUGHT IN THE AIR

Jesus told us all to watch
Don't sit around in despair
One day, we all will fly,
Caught up in the air

Can you imagine such a feeling,
All brothers and sisters in flight?
Will we have our hands outstretched?
Will it be morning, noon or night?

This will be the day of rapture
Have you made preparations to leave?
For He's coming as a thief in the night
Help us, God, to believe

Redemption comes through Jesus
As He displays His grace
It's not crowded; you can get in
Plenty of open space

As you pour out your heart to Him,
Desiring all His love to be exposed,
Can't you feel the Holy Ghost
As Jesus is saving your soul?

Later, no airplane ticket is needed
Jesus already has paid the fare
He's calling you up as you read,
Caught up in the air

Written 7-25-24 @ 7:30 a.m.

OUR HELP ON HIGH

We need directing, dear Lord,
As our focus is to apply,
Knowing that healing will come
From our help on high

As we pray, He will hear
We cry out to our King
As troubles come and then go,
We let Jesus know everything

Holding back nothing in prayer,
Explaining circumstances one by one,
Giving them all to these three,
Father, Holy Ghost and Son

As we disperse all problems,
Needing support to overcome,
He gives us strength to continue on,
For He does not just love some

He loves all who live
As we look at the things ahead,
We rely on guidance from Jesus
Spirits led and spirits fed

Looking forward through scripture,
Destination through the sky,
As we all focus on our Savior,
Our help on high

Written 7-26-24 @ 6 a.m.

To Overcome

As we are led by the Spirit,
Saying, *Lord Jesus, please come*
We are being stressed by trials
We need Your help to overcome

Guidance and deliverance are first
Protect us and set us free
Enlighten us in Your word
Help us accomplish what needs to be

We read to *Trust in the Lord*
Do good in all your ways
Delight thyself also in the Lord
In Him, commit your days

As we rejoice in salvation,
We sing praises to the lamb
Names He owns are the Prince of Peace,
Messiah, the great I am

With my whole heart, I will praise thee
I submit myself to You
Shelter me, Jesus, under Your wings
Carry me completely through

Scripture says serve You, the Lord,
To the end, when He does come
Give us strength and stability
With desire to overcome

Written 7-29-24 @ 5:30 a.m.

CONTROLLED BY LOVE

We seek after You, Lord
Help us move to You above
Give us directions to Your presence
In Your covenant controlled by love

Scripture says I must decrease,
That He will rise up in me
Praying for strength in my eyes
So that I might see

Have mercy upon me, o God
In humbleness do I bow
Help us, Jesus, to know righteousness
How to gain this, just how

You delivered me from death
As I was lost and undone,
But Your spirit revived me
Now, You and I are one

As I sing, giving You praise,
Casting all my care in His sight,
Making a joyful noise in the morning
That carries on through the night

Unto thee, o God, we give thanks
We delight ourselves in You above
We desire Your presence today
With submission controlled by love

Written 7-29-24, 6:15 a.m.

My Talent I Must Use

There is happiness in every soul
That accepts Jesus as Lord
Then Jesus declares them redeemed
And welcomes them aboard

Today is a whosoever will
We all have the ability to choose
Just like I'm doing right now
My talent I must use"

I write down on paper
As God's spirit sweeps my mind
I want my witness to be clear
As I let my light shine

Jesus still saves is the message
That's what the world needs to know
Then, as salvation is given,
By faith we grow

As scripture comes to light,
Darkness has been pushed away
No weapon formed will harm you
It's full speed ahead; no delay

I give honor and glory to our King
This gift I have, I can't lose
I look at what He's done for me
My talent I must use

Written 7-25-24 @ 5:40 a.m.

SCRIPTURE ABOUT THE CHURCH

We have statements in God's word
As I concluded my search,
It deals with a certain position:
Scripture about the church

You see, Paul wrote letters to her
Revelations calls her Christ's bride
Jesus purchased her with His blood
As a spear pierced His side

The truth is, she has a banner
It's displayed and also on file
Solomon saw her as a dove,
But one and undefiled

Jesus said she was built on a rock
Peter said peculiar people would join
Themselves with a perpetual covenant
To heaven is where they are going

You see, in 1903
June 13 was the day
The covering spread over was removed
Brother A.J. Tomlinson saw this way

There are many, many more statements
That categorize this so much
It takes a vision for the reader to see
Scripture about the church

Written 7-25-24 @ 5 a.m.

STEADFASTNESS IN HIM

In togetherness, we draw near,
For time is getting slim
Letting Jesus fulfill His work
Steadfastness in Him

His word keeps us stable
It blesses and directs our faith,
Protecting us from all harm,
Setting us free from His wrath

With divine intervention, we grow,
Being taught by Jesus Christ,
Listening closely to the Spirit,
Taking in all godly advice

We can do nothing without Him,
Needing understanding so that we see
That our jubilation will expand
What joy He gives to you and me

As we submit ourselves freely,
In our worship, teach us
We need wisdom to know better
In whom we should trust

We're dependent on You, Lord
Don't let our focus become dim
We are to magnify Your name
Steadfastness in Him

Written 7-29-24, 5 a.m.

PROVE ME NOW

How do you fathom God?
What is your definition of Him today?
When He tells you, *Prove me now*,
What exactly would you say?

Would you show gratitude and love
With your hands held high in praise?
Would you erase the pleasures of flesh
To acknowledge the pleasures of His ways?

There is happiness in serving God
As we walk, we let Him guide
Where He leads me, I will follow
So very close, side by side

Don't be afraid; move forward
Always remember this; just pray
When you're crossing that river of alligators,
Get in that wheelbarrow and stay

We praise You today, Lord Jesus
How wonderful is Your name
For You saved me through Your blood
Brought to me glory, leaving shame

So, as we travel in this life,
Seeking out the answer, the how,
We rely on scripture through the Spirit
When He tells us, *Prove me now*

Written 9-15-21, 5:30 a.m.

Captured But Now Free

I need everyone's attention
Are you as excited as me?
Think on this: Chains are gone
Captured but now free

As this reality sets in,
Glory to our King on high
Greatest achievement ever made
Deliverance — now, we testify

Now, we pursue godliness,
Desiring His precious word,
Praying that Jesus will supply,
Continuing in what we've heard

The Bible should be our resource
That we gather in as our guide
Moving forward is our objective,
Letting physical wants subside

We should know what we need
We've been enlightened by His grace
In knowing how He blesses us
Preparing to see Him face to face

Because He redeemed you and I,
Accepting our feeble pleas,
We have salvation through faith
    Captured but now free

Written 7-8-24, 8 a.m.

AS I LEARN, THEN I MOVE

My job is to follow Jesus
To continue in the groove
Revitalizing the Spirit inside
As I learn, then I move

Searching the scripture to see
If I'm securing my life
So priorities stay in line
That calmness replaces strife

Today is a solemn day
In His word, we all have hope
No matter the project ahead,
Through Jesus, we can cope

We pursue a new home
As the scripture comes to light
We cast away all doubt,
Securing knowledge of what's right

We've been given promises
From the King above Himself
Submission is what we must do
That we leave nothing left

Hallelujah to the lamb
Whatever is wrong in me, Lord, remove
For I need guidance today, Lord
As I learn, then I move

Written 7-14-24, 3:30 a.m.

WE CAN MAKE IT

How is your confidence level?
Is it high, medium or low?
Does your mindset need a lift,
Allowing positivity to grow?

Pausing all thoughts aside,
Small matters that won't stand
Saying, *We can make it*
Jesus declared that we can

For Jesus tells us in John,
Just ask it in my name,
And it shall be given to you
All we must do is claim

We can make it, He said
Follow me close; you'll see
No doubt inside this guide
He carries us, setting us free

In our walk, we proceed,
Moving deeper with the Lord
For it's joy that we feel,
Following Him in one accord

He washes us with His word
He cleans us, making us pure
Realizing we are in His hands
We can make it for sure

Written 12-6-23, 8 a.m.

HE LIVES

While you say, *Good morning, Jesus,*
Do you feel the joy He gives?
Since accepting Him as Lord,
Now inside of you, he lives

As you reminisce on life
And accomplishments you made,
What is one thing that stands out?
Made any major upgrades?

Jesus said, *Take up the cross*
Follow me, my precious child
Draw nigh to my protection,
Staying spotless and undefiled

Never forget what He did,
His life that was torn
Then, through repentance,
We would be reborn

In this dispensation of grace,
We bow before You, our King
We worship You in humility,
Thankful for the blessings You bring

How marvelous are Your works
You make our lives the best
We know this because He lives
Our souls have found rest

Written 12-6-23, 7:15 a.m.

CELEBRATING JESUS ON CHRISTMAS DAY

As we gather, we give honor
So many words we need to say
But the main words should be this:
Celebrating Jesus on Christmas Day

He's the reason for the season
Baby from Mary, the Virgin Mother
Child of Bethlehem, our King
He's the greatest of any other

The bread of life if you're hungry,
He gives salvation to the lost
He's the wonderful counselor Isaiah saw,
But His destination was to a cross

Crown of thorns placed on His head
Beaten and stabbed in the side
Have you given time to Him this morning?
Have you fallen down and cried?

He's the Savior of this world in which we are living
He's the transportation out of here
He gives grace and spreads it within

So, today, as we give honor,
We exalt Him as we pray
At His church, we are
Celebrating Jesus this Christmas Day

Written 12-4-23, 8 a.m.

ON BENDED KNEES

As I bow before you, Father,
Maker of land and all seas,
Let your spirit take control
As I ask on bended knees

For you know all things
There is nothing outside your reach
You're the lamb that came from above
You are our support here beneath

As we pray and seek your face,
Give us that divine direction
Help us to remember our promises
Send down to us correction

Create in us humbleness
As we travel life's weary road
Renew in us your power
To help us carry the load

Our help comes from you above
We live, we breathe because of you
As we decrease from ourselves,
We press forward to be made new

Knowledge and wisdom we pursue
With understanding to follow close
We need deliverance from obstacles
Guidance from the Holy Ghost

So, Heavenly Father, as I finish,
Remove from Zion this ease
In us, let your spirit reign
As I ask on bended knees

Written 4-14-05

FAVORITE SCRIPTURE

What's your favorite scripture?
Where is it found? What does it say?
Is it Old Testament, or New?
Does its meaning carry you away?

Psalms is a wonderful book
It declares so much inside,
Giving hope to the readers,
Making discouragement and doubt subside

Lean not unto thine own understanding
That's what Proverbs declares
Let's lean on the Maker of all
He freely gives and shares

Acts 17:28 tells us the story
None of us should be behooved
It tells us all that it's Jesus
In Him, we live and move

We owe it all to Him, my friend
Can we thank Him for what He's done?
Yes, He died for ,
And for all that, we could be one

The scriptures have life
They encourage and help you grow
So, today, what's your favorite scripture?
Read it; let it bless your soul

Written 10-1-18, 5 a.m.

Should Be Every Day

Tomorrow is a special time,
But really, I must say
In the spirit of Thanksgiving,
It should be every day

We should be thankful for life,
For all our family and friends
We should always feel gratitude
That Thanksgiving should not end

Life really is not life
If you're not on one accord
Life is really meaningless
Unless Jesus is your lord

For Thanksgiving comes from Him
He suffered anguish, along with pain
He purchased salvation through His death
Yes, the perfect lamb was slain

How He loved us, my friend
All He wants to do is please us
When you spend time thinking on Thanksgiving,
Spend some time thinking of Jesus

Does a tear form in your eye?
Words are hard to come by to say
Friend, when talking of Thanksgiving,
It Should be every day

WHY ME?

Why me? I said
With my head down low,
For yes, I feel unworthy
Of the blessings I've been bestowed

I have knowledge of the future
And what the future holds,
For I've received a vision
I watch as she unfolds

Yes, I say, *Why me?*
You should be saying it too
For the precious Son of God
Died for me and also you

Do you know this man personally?
And what knowing Him really meant?
He's the one who determines eternity
And where yours will be spent

I know this man myself
And I love Him more each day
But what direction are you headed?
Are you on that straight and narrow way?

All this that we've been given
Is it hard for you also to see?
And are you left with the words
Do you also wonder, *Why me?*

Written 6-13-15, Cemetery meeting

PRAISE TO THE FATHER ON HIGH

In life, we have privileges
As time slowly slips by
We're human beings with God's spirit
Praise to the Father on high

In this walk, we meet opposition
It causes stress and emotion
But I know a physician that heals
He is the perfect potion

As we open up the scripture,
Where should we look for direction?
Should it be about praising Him,
Or should we look for correction?

Either one of these will work
Correction and praise we both need
The kingdom of God is within us,
For we have received His seed

Free from corruption and sin
Redeemed by His blood and grace
He took all our trespasses in life
And all of them He did erase

We give Him glory and honor
As time slowly slips by
Can we all agree on this one fact:
Praise to the Father on high?

Written 2-27-24, 6:30 a.m.

NEITHER BE THOU DISMAYED

We are not held captive anymore
Our direction has already been laid.
We are secured in the arms of Jesus,
So neither be thou dismayed

On the pathway to heaven,
It's clear and so in view
We are being washed by His word
Cleansed, purified, made brand new

When we pass through the waters,
He said he would protect us all
Deliverance is inside His hands
There is no fear for any to fall

For as we walk, He guides
We lift our hands to Him in praise
For God said, *I am the Lord, thy God*
Follow me and trust me all of thy days

Jesus gave up His life
So that you and I could have more
Do you feel that love He shows?
It is truly something to adore

So much we have been given
So much because we have prayed
For He told us, *Rely upon me*
And neither be thou dismayed

Written 5-31-22, 7 a.m.

The Physician No One Seen

As the doctors all prepared
Everything so nice, so clean
Another doctor was also present,
The physician no one seen

He's a heart surgeon also
His technique so calm, so neat
All work He does is guaranteed
To make you all complete

As His spirit sweeps the body,
The Great Physician is His name
The son of God, the Prince of Peace,
Father, Holy Ghost, the same

He has to have no assistance
He has perfectness in His hands
He's the risen, Lord and Savior
He's the fairest inside this land

He is world-renowned throughout
His specialty is saving souls
He changes the lost to found,
The broken down to completely whole

Yes, I had no worries
The Great Physician was on the scene
For you see, it was our Jesus,
The physician no one seen

Written 8-21-2010

THE ONE WAY

When I'm driving the highway
And I see a *one way* sign,
I say in my heart, *Hallelujah*
For whom comes to mind

For I am the way, the truth and life
That's what my Savior said
I need all grounded in truth
To be spiritually fed

Don't let other ways distract
That lead to naught, wrong course
We need full speed ahead
Through Jesus, the right source

No other name was given
Whereby we must be saved
He came to earth to be a sacrifice
As His precious blood was gave

As we live today this life,
As we pursue life's great things,
Let's not forget the greatest gift:
To know and serve the king of kings

So, when you ride that highway,
There is one more thing I'd like to say
Let's all make sure that we know Jesus,
For he is truly the one way

2015 Jackson Family Reunion

Denied Although a Spotless Lamb

Happy birthday, Jesus
King of kings, the great I am
We celebrate this day because of You
Denied although a spotless lamb

Excuse me as I bow down
I praise You, oh mighty one
Help me to know all I need
That Your will in me will be done

Don't let me trust only in myself
And not look toward Your grace
Help me to seek Your favor
So I can look upon Your face

I desire to live by Your word,
Leaving all my thoughts behind
My plans are not here below
I'm on that upward climb

He gave His life for us all
The way of escape was laid
For Jesus, it meant crucifixion
The salvation plan era was made

Merry Christmas, everybody
It's because of the great I am
Give honor to Him, for he was
Denied although a spotless lamb

Written 12-25-2012

I Conquered It All For You

As we contemplate God's plan,
Our Jesus should come into view
These words should be declared:
I conquered it all for you

Being resurrected, He conquered death
The stone was rolled away
Tortured, shamed and killed,
But not a word did He say

Sent by His Father to this world
So that a sacrifice could be made
The king of kings for this human
Can you imagine such a trade?

He came to His own,
But His own people would not lay claim
To the precious lamb from heaven
The one name above all names

How great it is to know Him,
God's only begotten son
Have you spent time in His presence,
Thanking Him for all that He's done?

I plan on talking to Him shortly,
Pleading to Him that he'll come into view
For I believe in what He accomplished:
I conquered it all for you

If I Shut Up Heaven

As our joy does increase,
Within our mind, there's a stir,
For we all serve a Savior
How do all the blessings occur?

For our Father in Heaven,
Hallowed be thy name
All praises go to Him above
In this day, we proclaim

But what if blessings cease?
What if trials and tribulations did soar?
If God said, *I shut up Heaven*,
This life would be no more

For the trumpet had already sounded
The deadened Christ arose
They were on that plain air trip
Along with the alive, scripture shows

The bride had made herself ready
Total unity had made it within
When serving God, we have benefits
Nothing but win! Win! Win!

But God said, *If I shut up Heaven,*
No more blessings will occur
Let's, together, pray and fast
That will cause a spiritual stir

www.ingramcontent.com/pod-product-compliance
Lightning Source LLC
Chambersburg PA
CBHW061741070526
44585CB00024B/2765